Quick Guide V: How to Apply Mindfulness to Business Relationships

I0470981

Number 5 in a series of articles by

Paul C Burr PhD

http://paulcburr.com/

Acknowledgements

Steven Howard, Digital Marketing Strategist, Website SEO Writer, Marketing Consultant at *Howard Marketing Services*, Greater Los Angeles

Penelope Walsh, Writer and Editor

Terri Lofthouse MSc, Cognitive Behavioural Psychotherapist

Kelly Scales, Management Consultant and Entrepreneur

David Loxley, Chief Druid, *The Druid Order*, London

Titles in this Series

Other Books and Booklets by the Author

Contents

Preface

This article, in common with each of my other *Quick Guides to Business*, can be read quickly in less than an hour. It's also a workbook that you can then go through at your own pace to complete the exercises herein.

The contents bear from my research, consulting, direct selling and coaching within global corporations over a twenty year period. The companies I worked directly for, or in a freelance capacity with, include: IBM, Cisco, Accenture, Xerox, Microsoft, American Express, Standard Chartered, BP and Reckitt Benckiser. During this period I've had the privilege to meet and work with hundreds of top performers worldwide.

This has proven the most challenging booklet to write so far in the series of *Quick Guides to Business*. It contrasts...

1. My experience of what top performers in business do differently from moderate performers.
2. The rapidly emerging science of *Mindfulness*, as practiced by *Cognitive Behavioural Therapy* (*CBT*) psychotherapists.
3. Ancient wisdom: the understanding and playing of the *Game of Life* as practiced by Ancient Egyptians.

With

4. Druidic wisdom combined with impeccable research into the purpose of and functioning of an entity known as *The Master Mind* (or *Group Spirit*) that exists between two or more people in a group (Ref: *The Law of Success* and *Think and Grow Rich* by Napoleon Hill).

I learned that the same principles from all four sources apply cohesively to the same behaviours and practices that top performers engage in to overcome the setbacks that business, life and the future send our way.

I do not imply that you have to believe in my work, *CBT*, ancient or druidic wisdom. I ask that you simply practice it, to prove its utility for yourself.

Paul C Burr

September 2013

Overview

When you give a top performer a target to aim for, they look beyond the target. Top performers stretch themselves. They set a range of targets. The minimum being 'success' as defined by others. Success is their target but their purpose is to be the best, and often be seen to be the best. Top performers seek fulfilment through a sense of *completeness* that they have acknowledged and dealt with everything that is 'incomplete' in their approach to business - specifically business relationships.

The Journey to Completeness (a '10 out of 10')

The *journey to completeness* is a step-by-step process. Each step has both intellectual and emotional content. Getting a top performer to raise their game from say a 7 out of 10 (which is the median score top performers give themselves) to a 10 out of 10 (where 10 is "perfect") is a two-stage process.

1. Going from a 7 to an 8 out of 10 is a straight-forward and, by-and-large, an intellectual process. We can all work a little smarter. (If a coach can't help you achieve a one point improvement in your effectiveness, find another coach!)
2. Going from an 8 to 9 to 10 is an emotional journey. The journey is filled with limiting (or disabling) beliefs 'you' (by 'you' I mean you, me, we, us) hold about yourself. If creating superior business

relationships was purely an intellectual process (e.g. create the best business case and it will sell itself) then smart people, especially top performers, would already be there. The journey from 8 to 10 is an emotional journey that requires you to sit in and gauge the feeling of where you are right now, in the present moment. Specifically, you sense and deal with any fear that exists in you or the person with whom you're forging a business relationship. Over time, you develop a more intuitive approach to business relationships, through *mindfulness*.

Intu(n)ition

Top performers spend more time developing wisdom intuitively and, more importantly, they apply it. They learn (better than moderate performers) wisdom from their innermost fears and summon the courage to release (as opposed to conquer) those fears.

Sidenote: Courage is a choice, not the trait of a privileged few. We all have courage. In certain circumstances, we choose not to use it. I include me in the 'we'!

Moderate or less effective performers (who are equal in honour but not privilege with top performers) are, by definition, less motivated, less confident, less competent and/or less curious to learn - than top performers.

Effectiveness = Motivation x Confidence x Competence x Curiosity

Or

$$E = MC^3$$

(Ref: Quick *Guide II - How to Spot, Mimic and Become a Top Salesperson*)

If we feel less motivated, less confident or less competent than our peers, understandably we will be less curious to sit in that feeling for long. If we feel lacking, our resilience to fear may well be lower. We allow any strife, especially in a key business relationship, to have a more poignant effect on ourselves.

Yet strife in a relationship serves a purpose...

Everything that irritates us about others can lead us to an understanding of ourselves.
Carl Jung

I would add to Dr Jung's quotation, *"and a better understanding of our fears"*. And if we don't spend time seeking and acknowledging our innermost fears, we may find ourselves mimicking moderate performers.

Moderate performers spend more time either

1. Distracting themselves from their fears by being seen to be busy. *You cannot release what you deny yourself to possess.*

And/or

2. Feeding their fears (often of failure or perceived incompetence). They spend their time keeping a low profile; taking few risks. Like birds, they fly and do their best to keep up with the flock. As long as they don't stick out from the rest then they hope that they won't be singled out to account for themselves. Think of this as the *"They can't sack everybody"* syndrome.

Either way, moderate performers allow their 'incompleteness' to travel into the past (see subheading, **Ancient Wisdom**, later in this section) only to return to the future. Whereas top performers demonstrate a superior amount of *faith-in-self* to tune into what's going on inside of them and listen to what the 'little voice of intuition' has to say.

Intuition + Tune in to self = Intunition

Think of *intunition* as a tuning knob on an old fashioned radio device. You turn it to tune into the present tense, a radio station called...

Mindfulness

Mindfulness means moment-to-moment, non-judgmental awareness. It is cultivated by refining our capacity to pay attention, intentionally, in the present moment, and then sustaining that attention over time as best we can. In the process, we become more in touch with our life as it is unfolding.
Jon Kabat-Zinn

Allow me to add my own business related definition.

Mindfulness is responding in the present moment without reacting through anger, shame, hurt or (the most likely feeling) fear. Instead it's about having faith-in-self to use your intuition to respond with passion, curiosity to learn, composure, patience, compassion, harmony, and timing to complete whatever is incomplete in your approach to business relationships.

Responding to what or whom? Answer - to whatever 'the future' brings to you in the present moment. And one of the future's gifts to you is everything that is incomplete in your approach to business relationships. For example, I've coached several senior and very successful business executives who have 'a ceiling' to the business circles they feel comfortable keeping. One high ranking partner in a consulting firm felt uncomfortable in the presence of CEO's when their boss was also present, another shied away from mixing with 'captains' of their industry, another would bully people and respond angrily to situations that they couldn't 'control'. A managing partner of a law firm felt uncomfortable meeting employees at the client interface. All four, by the way, were more than capable intellectually of holding their own (without feeling fearful or upset) and bringing value to such encounters.

Mindfulness in various guises has been around for thousands of years.

Ancient Wisdom

Mindfulness in psychology is a relatively new term. But the practise of *mindfulness*, perhaps in more abstract terms, was well understood by the Ancient Egyptians, some 3000 years BCE.

The illustration on the next page, *The Sun Boat travelling between the future and the past*, is the cover of a booklet, *The Life Game, No 2,* from a series of meditation texts on Druidic wisdom, created by David Loxley, Chief Druid, *The Druid Order*, London.

As you travel in the present, the future brings you wisdom of whatever is incomplete within you. It brings you people, events, situations that in the past have caused you to react through anger, hurt, shame or fear. Instead of allowing these negative emotions to take hold of you; by not reacting or purposefully under-reacting, you give yourself the opportunity to reflect, look within and learn what it is inside you that attracts the type of upsetting event you face.

Should you learn and apply the wisdom 'mindfully' (i.e. complete what is incomplete), the event goes into the past and need never return. Should you react and cloud yourself in a negative emotion, you cannot see within - literally and metaphorically - to help yourself. Nor can anyone else. The event goes into the past and returns to the future in a similar form; only to return again and again until you choose to stop and react differently - by under-reacting and adopting a mindful approach to the situation.

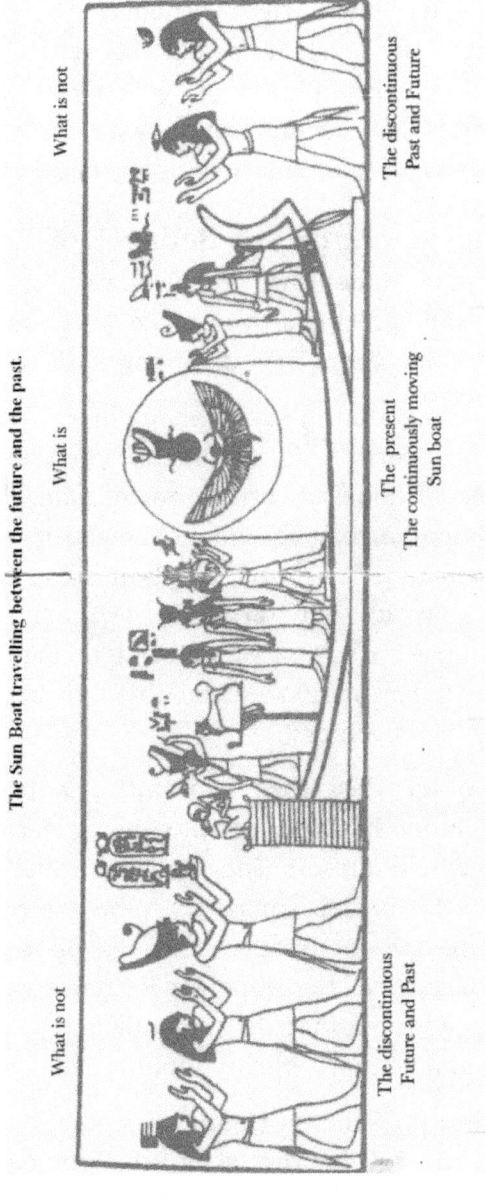

The Sun Boat travelling between the future and the past.

What is not

What is

What is not

The discontinuous
Past and Future

The present
The continuously moving
Sun boat

The discontinuous
Future and Past

Whether you're into ancient wisdom or not, at a logical and pragmatic level it makes sense to improve whatever needs improving (complete what is incomplete) in your approach to business relationships; to create more harmony or resonance.

Build Agreements on a Bedrock of Truth

One further dimension to business relationships concerns the agreements you make with yourself and others. Are they borne of truth or not-truth, i.e. fear?

Truth in a relationship starts when illusion stops. Only truth brings forth true happiness, albeit eventually. Not-truth, dishonesty, brings forth pain. In every relationship, you have a simple choice: truth or not-truth, happiness or pain. Relationships make the business world go around. Without trusting relationships based on truthful agreements there would be no harmony. You would neither buy nor sell anything - 'not business'.

This booklet describes a mindful approach to building more harmonious business relationships, starting with yourself. They will be profitable. They have to be for business partners to be happy, do they not? There are mountains of books on developing strong business relationships. I've written some myself. This is a book of that ilk yet with a much deeper, different and far more effective approach.

It describes the mindful (thoughts + emotions) stages by which you develop the relationship you have firstly with yourself. Once you are in the right frame of *mindfulness*, you send out a signal that contains *faith-in self, passion, curiosity to learn, composure, patience, compassion* and hopefully *'completeness'*. You can then attract the success you seek wholly. Because...

You attract the same qualities in others as those you send out.

Extremists and Non-extremists

You meet two categories of people; those with extreme views (my observation, about 15% minority) and those without (85% majority). By and large, it's the extremists, especially those outside the norms of behaviour, who change things. Extremists have opposers. Followers and laggards have none as they push for very little.

Thus, when you're relating to an extremist, they may well need help. People with extreme views, be they positive or negative, are relatively easy to spot. They'll either be very encouraging and passionate about what you're saying or doing - OR they'll tire, show their frustration and perhaps withdraw from any interaction with you quickly.

People without extreme views may appear easier to get along with. The question mark remains, is their lack of extremism a sign of maturity; a balanced view - or - is it an unwillingness to 'stick their head above the parapet' for fear of it being shot? The self coaching tools in this booklet and lines of questioning will help you find out.

This assumes that your business relationship operates in a relatively egalitarian environment. Company politicking stifles truth. And without truth, you conduct business in denial or ignorance.

Technology (e.g. the Internet) is hastening the age of truth in business and politics.

Truth is the new currency that top performers don't shirk away from.

Part of 'your truth' is the negative patterns in your behaviours noticed by others that you personally are unaware of. Behind these, and more fundamentally, you'll find unconscious subroutines, *limiting core beliefs* and *dysfunctional assumptions*, that trigger these negative patterns of behaviour - borne of anger, shame, hurt or (in most cases) fear. We all have them. I have not met anyone who doesn't have at least one.

This is the future's gift to the present moment; to transform the negative into positive; the opportunity to discover and complete everything that is incomplete in your business approach to relationships. Profit, wealth and fame may be your external goals BUT I discovered that 'real top performers' want something more.

They want to know what it takes to be the very best at what they do. Which means not only do they seek; they embrace the future's presents (wisdom of incompletions) moment by moment. Theirs is a far richer definition of business life. Top performers see business as a process of *consciousness development* (even though they don't call it this) much akin to the way Ancient Egyptians viewed the world.

Hierarchy of Values - Exercise

"People like people like themselves." For you to influence someone; they, at some level, will need to approve of you - and vice versa. They will notice if and how what appears important to you is congruent with what is important to them - or, at the very least, you are respectful of what's important to them, their values.

Values are things you demonstrate because they influence your traits, characteristics and behaviour. You imply what's important to you.

(From which...)

If you don't make your values clear, others infer them - and they might infer them incorrectly. As might you, should you assume you know their values.

You have some priority as to what's important to you, your *hierarchy of values*. If your hierarchy is similar to those you seek to influence then all well and good. If not, then you may have some flexing to your repertoire, of how you come across, to be done.

———

Exercise...

As you think about a specific business relationship (or potential for a relationship) and the context in which you find yourself, what's important to you (i.e. your values)?

Make a list; write down everything that's important to you. As you look at each item, what's one word or phrase that describes what you've written? For example if 'seeing the relationship working' is important, you could characterise this phrase with the term, *security*. Here are some further client-examples of values: *achievement, planning, strategy, relationships, facts and logic, entrepreneurship, trust, a scientific approach, a step-by-step approach, an elegant approach, a people oriented approach, logic and reasoning, problem resolution, big picture, attention to detail, collaboration, fun, instinct, data analysis,* and so on.

By way of example, here's a simple technique to determine your *hierarchy of values.* Imagine four values: *achievement, proven process, strategic positioning* and *relationships.* Write down each value on a small piece of paper. Ask yourself...

If I could have only one of either achievement or a proven process, which would I choose?

By way of example I give my answers. I stress they are not your answers. There are no rights and wrongs here. I speak of preferences, not rights or wrongs.

My answer is *achievement* (you can substitute your real answers, once you see how the exercise works). So I place *achievement* (as current no. 1) above *proven process* (currently allocated as no. 2).

I.e. My 'work in progress' *hierarchy of values* is...

1. *Achievement*
2. *Proven process*

Now ask...

If I could have only one of either strategic positioning or proven process (current no. 2) *which would I choose?* I put *strategic positioning* as more important; this now becomes my no. 2 with *proven process* now in lowest place as no. 3. I repeat the question to compare the importance I place between (1) *achievement* and (2) *strategic positioning*. *Achievement* still comes out on top. So my revised *hierarchy of values* becomes...

1. *Achievement*
2. *Strategic positioning*
3. *Proven process*

Now ask...

If I could have only one of either relationships or proven process which would I choose? My answer is *relationships*. Likewise when I compare the importance of relationships with strategic positioning and subsequently achievement, it comes first both times. (Yes, it's obvious, I place relationships above everything in business.) So my finalised and personal *hierarchy of values* is...

1. *Relationships*
2. *Achievement*

3. *Strategic positioning*
4. *Proven process*

You can now integrate a further value into your *hierarchy of values* (e.g. *facts and data*) by starting from the bottom up and contrast it with each value (i.e. *proven process, strategic positioning, achievement* and *relationships* in that sequence) and raise the new value by one until you reach an existing value that has higher priority.

――――

Case Study: Head of Training and Development in UK for a Top Global Software Company

My (yet to be) coaching client presented her recommendations for her company's annual training and development plan to the UK managing director. She presented the facts and data behind the business case to achieve the plan (*achievement*) along with details of how it would be implemented (*proven process*).

The managing director queried how the plan integrated with US's plans and had her US counterpart seen the UK plan. He instructed the Training and Development Director to get feedback from US. On her return, he then inquired as how she proposed to get the sales force's buy in to spending time away from work. Did she have the support of the regional sales managers? Off she went again and returned a second time to get the final sign off she sought.

Almost a year later I introduced my (by then) client to the following quadrant of categories of values...

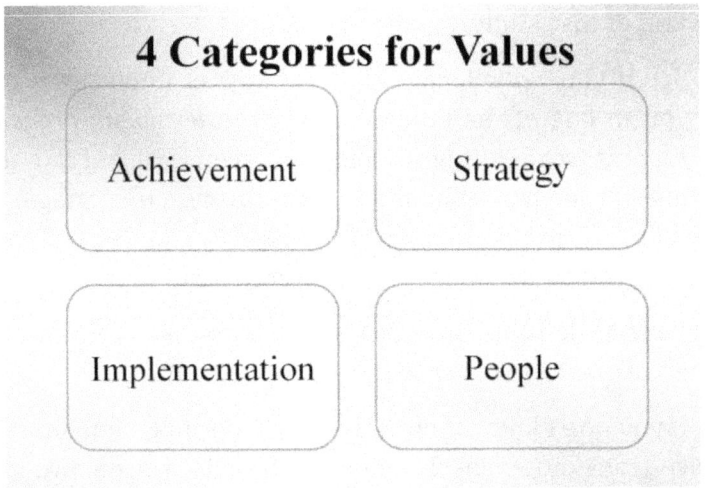

As soon as she saw the quadrant, she recognised that the managing director was a 'natural flexer'; he looked at all proposals through four 'looking glasses' (*achievement, strategic positioning, proven process* and *relationships*).

In her next annual presentation, she started by saying, "You can look at this training plan from four perspectives...

1. The facts and data that support the business case for its achievement
2. Details of the roll out plan using proven processes
3. How it dovetails in with the global training plan
4. People's buy in to commit to the plan.

Where would you like me to start?"

My client was in and out of the one hour presentation with it signed off within twenty minutes.

End of case study_____

See if you can allocate all the things of importance to you in one of the four quadrants *achievement, proven process, strategic positioning,* or *relationships.* If one doesn't seem to fit in any of these, place it in a category called, *Other.* You now have hopefully a better feel for how you demonstrate your preferences to others.

Your task is to find theirs and flex your repertoire accordingly, in order to influence them.

If you don't know their thinking preferences, find out. If you do know, check anyway. Here is a sequence of searching questions to ask, once you have someone's permission to ask them.

1. *As you think about 'this project' and go into the future, how will you know you're being successful? Over and above external measures, how else will you know that it's been a success?*
2. *What changes are going on (or might go on) that (might) somehow affect the success of this project?*
3. *And as you think about where you are now, what's working well and what would you like to improve or change?*
4. *If you were to summarise what you've said so far, what are the top two or three things of importance to you, concerning 'this project'?*

The four questions should inform you of the other person's *hierarchy of values* - and thus the wisdom of where and how to focus your language patterns when you discuss 'the project' with them.

You can keep your wisdom up to date with the following question, *"May I ask, what, if anything, has changed your thinking about the project since we last met?"*

And remember...

> *Wisdom is only of value when you apply it!*

End of exercise _____

By now you hopefully have clear understanding of what's important to you and the person you wish to collaborate with and influence. Values set the overriding tone to your relationship. They are partly based on where you are now. And now, this very moment, is where you meet the future - for it presents the present with wisdom. More on this later.

Facts, Feelings and Imagery to Spark Ideas and Develop Intuition

People's views of the same situation can differ because they...

1. Start from a different place
2. Use different logic, facts and data
3. Differ in their purpose or vision of the future

4. Have differing views about what's important (*hierarchy of values* - covered in the previous chapter)
5. Have different levels of fear about the risks involved.

I focused on harmonising all the above points in the two preceding booklets in this series, *Quick Guide III: How to Bridge the Pillars of Successful Business Relationships* and *Quick Guide IV: A Scorecard that Accounts for Mindfulness in Business*. In this chapter, I introduce an exercise to develop your intuitive approach to improving your business relationship.

This exercise takes a snapshot of the dynamics of your business relationship, at any moment in time, at three levels...

1. Facts ... intellectual
2. Feelings... emotional or mental
3. Imagery... identity or intuitional

The intuitive mind is a sacred gift and the rational mind is a faithful servant. We have created a society that honours the servant and has forgotten the gift.
Albert Einstein

By way of example, here's an anonymous client case study of a CEO for a medium sized UK training company.

———

Case Study: 'Shapeshifting' to Get a Winning Result

My client was embroiled head-to-head with a major competitor to win a contract for a UK wide training solution. These were 'her' facts at the time...

Facts...

1. *Neither she nor the competitor had a 'total solution'. Her company had "great content", better than her competitor's and the buyer acknowledged this. The competitor had a superior nationwide network of proven trainers.*
2. *The buyer was introducing risk clauses into the contract which made it less economically viable.*
3. *Time was pressing because the buyer had deadlines to meet and it would take my client too long to recruit the trainers she needed to fulfil the terms of the contract.*

I then got my client to list all the feelings she associated with the above facts.

Feelings:

- *Concerned that the window of opportunity was closing.*
- *Concerned that the contract was becoming less profitable by the day.*
- *At a loss about what to do next.*

Next I asked the client to consider the facts and sit in the feelings she associated with the facts.

I asked, "Place yourself in a picture with the facts and feelings present. What image of yourself do you conjure?"

My client answered, "A builder of a half complete pyramid without the necessary resources to complete it".

Now it happened that in a previous coaching session I'd asked the client to go into the future and see herself with all the successes she wished for herself and her company. I asked her what image was she seeing herself as in this picture of success. She answered, *"A wise panther"*. (You can do this easily for yourself by using the methodology used so far in this case study, to describe the facts and feelings of what 'total success' would look like for you in the future. As you sit in this picture of success, what image of yourself do you conjure?)

I used the image of a *wise panther* to spark an intuitive idea in the client's mind. I asked the client, "So what would a *wise panther* do in this situation?" ....

Later that afternoon my CEO client made a telephone call. The next morning she journeyed two hundred miles north for a meeting with the CEO of her competitor at 11am. By 3pm, they had collaborated on a solution that made best use of both company's resources and training content. They called the buyer together with a proposal to combine forces. A profitable deal was struck within a week. Result!

End of Case Study_____

Exercise

- Use the above *Facts, Feelings and Imagery* methodology to conjure an image of yourself being totally successful in everything you do.
  - Write down what it is about this image that makes you so successful.

    (For example, in the instance of my client's *wise panther*, she cited...

    - *Agile and lithe, ready to move quickly*
    - *Can climb to get a treetop view of everything that's going on around me*
    - *Can judge distances and timings perfectly*
    - *Can blend in unseen in the background*
    - *Use my experience to achieve goals with minimum effort)*

- Focus on the important business relationship you wish to improve.
- Start by listing all the facts that have influenced or continue to influence the relationship for you and the other person(s) involved.
- List all the feelings you associate with each fact.
- What image of yourself do the facts and feelings conjure?
- Now list all the feelings that the person you're trying to influence associates with each of the facts. If you're uncertain, find out as best you can.
- What image do you conjure of the other person?
- How does the image of the other person relate to your image? Where is there resonance or harmony between

21

you? Where is there dissonance, tension, stress, or conflict?

- Write down all things you can do more of or differently to improve the harmony, passion and sense of security in the relationship.
- Write down all the things you can do more of or differently to ease any tension or harmonise any dissonance.

For a comprehensive coaching tool to raise people's passion and sense of security in a relationship, refer to the section *Thrive, Survive or Crumble* in *Quick Guide III: How to Bridge the Pillars of Successful Relationships*.

The previous case study illustrates the power of using imagery mindfully to foster creativity - i.e. making a connection between two things that wasn't there before; in this instance, a business problem and the image of *a wise panther.*

Creativity comes from making connections between disparate things where no perceived connection existed prior - i.e. you create something out of what was perceived as nothing.
(Part borrowed)

First you have to be mindful of the facts and sit in the (present tense) feeling of the situation at length. You need to combine faith-in self, passion, curiosity to learn, composure, patience, and compassion, to connect the dots of the unknown.

Build Outcomes - Exercise

This section will help you develop outcomes mindfully for your business relationship, through a balanced exchange of energy between you and the person you're dealing with.

Track Your Commitment

Bring into focus how your relationship has been of late. Answer and write down the answers to the following questions and responses to instructions...

- *Give yourself a score of 0 to 10 for level of satisfaction with the relationship where 10 equates to 100% - "The relationship is exactly how I want it to be", 5 equates to "Half and half" or "So so", 0 equates to "Not at all" and so on.*
- *What has been your input to making the relationship how you want it to be?*
- *Give yourself a score of 0 to 10 for your level of commitment to the relationship where 10 equates to 100%, 5 equates to 50%, 0 equates to nothing at all and so on.*
- *Track your level of commitment to the relationship on a weekly basis.*

You raise your level of commitment by raising how much (energy) you give to and receive from the relationship materially, mentally, emotionally and spiritually - as long as what you give or receive is not borne of anger, hurt, shame, or fear.

The relationship is in balance when you receive the same amount of 'energy' as you give. When a business relationship gets to exactly where both parties want it to be, both rate their satisfaction with it as a '10'. A '10 all round' is where both parties are fully committed to the relationship, they both give and receive 100% ('second best' is neither given nor received) which means they are both 100% satisfied.

Giving/Receiving - *Mindfulness*, Thought-guidance Exercise

Make notes and write down answers to questions as you work though the following thought-guidance exercise.

Close your eyes and take three conscious breaths, count 1 to 4 on each in-breath and out-breath with a short comfortable pause between each inhalation and exhalation. On each in-breath, imagine breathing in warmth and relaxation. On each out-breath imagine exhaling all tension and troubles of the day. Breathe in the 'present', breathe out the 'past'.

Now allow your breathing to become shallow, regular and comfortable.

Answer the following:

How has your relationship been of late?

What level of commitment to the relationship would you score yourself (out of 10)? (Remember commitment does not include any thoughts, deeds or words spoken borne out of anger, hurt, shame, or fear. If anything, they have a negating effect.).

Now think of a time when you were with someone or a group of people and you were being exactly as you wanted to be, you expressed your true nature free from any hindrance and they expressed theirs. Put yourself back in that situation, see yourself and the person (or people) with you, hear the things you said, listen to what they said in reply, imagine sitting in that feeling again, right now.

What was it that you shared that made you feel so good? What did you give? What did you receive? Relive that feeling. Turn up the brightness, colours, sounds, or feelings to a state where maximum joy and wisdom are shared.

And now turn your attention to your existing relationship. Remember the phrase, "Look after yourself so that you can look after others", as you answer the following.

- *What would the other business person most like to receive from you?*
- *Imagine giving it.*
- *Imagine their response.*
- *Is there something you would want in return?*
- *Would you want this something first?*

Outcomes

So now, write down the outcomes of giving and receiving exactly what you want from the relationship. Focus on the outcomes and park any limiting beliefs (about yourself, the other person or the journey ahead) you may hold that once stood in your way.

Note: A limiting belief is any sustained thought borne out of anger, hurt, shame, or fear.

———

Client Case Study - Hi-tech Sales

A coaching client of mine was in the midst of a sales campaign. She was trying to persuade the IT Architect to install an automated software management solution, to reduce running costs and improve the effectiveness of running a UK bank's computer network.

The business case was sound and the technology was proven in the USA but not the UK, as the technology had only just then been introduced into Europe. The customer was balking at the deal when my client brought her problem to one of our coaching sessions.

Prior to taking my client through the above thought-guidance exercise I asked...

What are the 2-3 most important facts or things going on in the mind of your client, about your proposal?

Back came the answer...

1. *My customer is nervous about committing to new technology in what is a core management function which is his responsibility. The last time he installed some new software it backfired and caused him a lot of embarrassment.*
2. *The amount of investment is not insignificant and would require board authority. Thus exposing my client's position as being accountable for the success of the project.*

3. *(As an aside but proved significant) My client wants to get fit again so he can coach his son to play rugby.*

I then used some short-cut questions to take my client through the above thought-guidance process...

- *How does your sales proposal, as is, match the facts and feelings your client has about it?*
- *What would they need to receive from you to allay their fears?*
- *What could you offer them harmoniously, to improve their passion and commitment to your proposition?*

I then took my client through the 'complete thought-guidance' process. After the coaching session she reviewed all her answers to the questions I'd asked, and crafted a deal that she felt would have more 'traction' with her client.

1. She took the risk out of her proposal by offering a low-cost pilot solution. If the project was a success, her client would get the credit; if not, then board presentations could be couched so that her sales organisation would 'foot the embarrassment'.
2. If the project was a complete failure, the equipment would be taken away free of charge.
3. She designed a solution which when implemented would free up the IT Architect's time by up to two hours a day. This would allow

her customer to take time out to get himself fit so that he could spend more time with his son.

As is often the case, the solution to my client's sales problem was not rocket science. All she needed was the *mindfulness*, by answering simply crafted questions about giving and receiving, to create the pathway through to a win-win scenario for both she and her client.

(End of case study)_____

Approval, Blocks, Leaks and Self Esteem

In order for anyone else to influence you, you need to 'approve' of them first, i.e. have sufficient trust in their integrity, capability and the value they bring to 'the table you share with them'. Likewise anyone else will need to approve of you before they allow you to influence them.

Influence and approval are forms of giving and receiving with a person. They receive the influence you 'give' them be it advice, guidance or support because they give you their approval. Likewise you agree (or not) to receive their influence because you give them your approval (or not).

What else stops giving and receiving? Answer: *blocks* and *leaks*.

A *block* occurs when you or your business partner will only give or receive so much, e.g. attention, passion, honesty, support, advice, guidance, material resources.

A *leak* occurs when you or your business partner divert your attention elsewhere from the task in hand, e.g. day-to-day business issues, politicking or any distraction that diverts your attention away from giving and receiving.

At some level, most of us have *blocks* and *leaks* with just about everyone we meet.

Some questions to ask are:

1. *Is the business transaction (i.e. the giving and receiving) you are conducting equitable?*
2. *Is the relationship sustainable (e.g. is one of you allowing the chaos that can happen in business to divert you away from the task in hand, rather than setting up 'mental boundaries' to keep your head focused)?*
3. *Are both parties satisfied? Or does one or both want to give or receive more?*

And if the answer to any of the above is "no" then your outcome should also address the lack of harmony ('business speak' in recent years often uses the term 'resonance') that exists.

> *Lack of harmony is the first, and often the last and only, cause of FAILURE.*
> From *The Law of Success*, by Napoleon Hill

The 'wheel of giving and receiving' needs a lubricant. The main ingredient of which is *faith-in-self* (or *self-trust/esteem*). People with a healthy level of *faith-in self* acknowledge their vulnerabilities (i.e. sources of anger, hurt, shame, and fear) and are okay with them. (Ref: *www.ted.com/talks/lang/eng/brene_brown_on_vulnera bility.html* by Brene Brown.)

Your *journey to success* starts by raising your *faith-in-self* to a level where you ready yourself to practise: *curiosity, composure, sensibility, co-opting others, inspiration, passion,* and *complete learning.* (I cover all but the last of these *key traits and characteristics of top performers* in the booklet, *Quick Guide II: How to Spot, Mimic and Becaome a Top Salesperson.* I define *complete learning* in the next section, *The Business Game of Complete Learning.*)

(For help on raising your *faith-in-self,* refer to *Seven Tools for Living Day to Day Life More Wisely,* page 178, *Step 3: Create the Context in Which to Succeed,* from my book, *Learn to Love and Be Loved in Return.*)

It's not the winning that counts, it's how you play the game...

If you're in a business relationship, you are already playing a game. Although the circumstances and the consequences of the game can be huge and rewarding or severe and tragic, it is a game - the *business game.*

In my youth, I often heard the axiom (usually when the English national football team were defeated by another nation who had a tendency to play outside the spirit of the 'English way'), *"It's not the winning that counts, it's how you play the game".* With so much money, prestige and influence in the media to 'win at all costs' associated with professional sport these days, I haven't heard the axiom used in decades.

Well now it's back because the *business game* is about 'how you play'. And the 'how you play' determines how much you move towards a top performer's purpose for the *business game*; which is ultimately about 'releasing' that which you allow to hold yourself back.

A top performer's goal is to win and their purpose is fulfilment...

...much akin to the way Ancient Egyptians viewed the world.

The Business Game of 'Complete Learning'

(Adapted from' *Quick Guide IV – A Scorecard that Accounts for Mindfulness in Business.)*

Your purpose is more than to succeed. It is to learn and apply the wisdom needed to succeed.

A mutually beneficial and financial rewarding business relationship might be your goal, but 'business' is the time and space that happens between now and reaching that goal. You attract the future that comes towards you. The future presents you with what remains incomplete right now in your business approach. The future presents the present with the opportunity to learn about yourself (conscious and especially sub-conscious sources of anger, hurt, shame, and fear), incomplete wisdom - AND apply the wisdom gleaned to release what's incomplete – *completeness*. Should you complete what is incomplete, it travels into the past and need not return.

Whatever travels into the past that remains incomplete 'returns to the future'. Whatever issues (i.e. unlearned or unapplied wisdom) that remain incomplete, be they business or personal, return again and again until you complete them. You know something is incomplete when you have allowed any residual anger, hurt, shame, or fear to control your thoughts, deeds or words.

When you start something, 'complete' it - which means...

Include Everything, Success and Not-success

Let's say you're in a competitive bid to win a sales campaign and the customer has objections (some of which might be hidden from you) to your proposal. If you attempt to deny the customer's right to air their objections by ignoring them or arguing with the customer about the fallacy of their logic or perception, you undervalue your bid. If, on the other hand, you seek out any hidden objection but fear to handle it, (i.e. you fear to... reframe any customer misperceptions or resolve genuine problems with, and counterbalance genuine drawbacks to, your proposal) then you allow the objection to take control of the sales situation, i.e. you allow fear to control your actions and that fear can spread to the customer. If you allow fear to seize control, you can end up doing nothing, perhaps like 'a rabbit caught in headlights'. Your sales proposal may thus be regarded as 'incomplete' in the value it offers.

The duality [you can't know any 'thing' without knowing or having the 'not-thing' adjacent to it, e.g. wet and not-wet/dry, success and not-success/failure (I prefer to use the term 'setback')] of life applies to business. So 'completing' the journey to success requires that you seek out all that is incomplete - and, for starters, this requires the following subset of qualities and attributes...

- *Faith-in-self* - trust your intuition especially when a lack of data is available.
- *Curiosity (to learn)* - to unearth all the hidden issues that bar your way to success.
- *Passion* - for the journey, the game; success is but a fleeting moment and anyway (if I may speak 'tongue-in-cheek'), *"the half life of senior management appreciation is about five minutes"*.
- *Composure* - is really about under-reacting to even the largest business crisis you face; it's about being cool and focused on the inside as well as in appearance.
- *Timing* - comes when everything is 'complete'. There's a time to 'keep your powder dry' and a time to 'fire'.

And

- *Harmony* or *resonance* - you're in tune with your business partner's innermost wants and fears - and they are in tune with yours.

Ask all the questions I've listed in this booklet so far and you will demonstrate your *curiosity* and *passion* for what your relationship is about. Handle issues and objections openly and honestly, and you will demonstrate *faith-in-self*. Let's move on to *composure* and *timing*.

When you go for a big business deal, the bigger the deal, the more unknowns there are. The more unknowns there are, the bigger the risk involved. The bigger the risk involved, the more trust is required: trust in personal or organisational integrity, capability, disaster recovery, contract, technology, and, perhaps most important of all, *faith-in-self* by all concerned. (For more information on the dimensions of trust, refer to the first booklet in this series, *Quick Guide - How Top Salespeople Sell*.)

Trust is the gap between what you know and what you place faith in.

The closer you get to the deal (success), the closer you get to losing the deal (not-success). This is the time that composure or lack of composure has its most poignant effect.

———

Case Study, Lack of Composure:

A sales/engineering team spent two years (and their company had invested millions of pounds) in attempting to win a vast IT outsourcing deal. The team was favoured to win but there were *"one or two important things to iron out"*. During the week running up to the 'decision day', one or two team members would visit the bathroom on arrival at work and literally throw up. They felt their careers were on the line. Despite putting on a brave front, they were doing all the last minute negotiations in a state of inner panic. Alas, the customer picked up on the vibration of their nervousness and became uncomfortable.

The customer felt that the sales team was trying to avoid certain 'grey areas' in the deal. When the customer discussed these 'grey areas' with the sales team's competitor, they got a whole and composed response. You can guess what happened.

End of case study_____

As you get close to success, there's a temptation to avoid learning about everything that will stop success. The fear of unearthing something you don't want to hear, something too great to contemplate. Instead, you ignore the warning signs. You ignore the little voice in your stomach that says *"something's wrong"*. The simple message is ***"Don't! Practice faith-in-self!"*** Remain mindful.

Include both success and not-success in your quest. Welcome all the things (incompletions) that will stop you succeeding. Want them. Seek them and they will present themselves to you...

1. Check your intentions, moment by moment. As a famous film line goes, *"Are you listening or are you waiting to talk?"*
2. Avoid reacting out of anger, shame, hurt, and most of all fear. Avoid panic: instead, under-react, 'park' your fears.
3. Avoid denying your fears' existence, allow them to be, 'shine light' on them.

Fears are not to be conquered, they are to be released.

You cannot release what you deny yourself to possess.

4. Imagine how you want those that you deal with to be - that's the 'vibe' to put out. Practise, for example, *faith-in-self, passion, curiosity to learn what needs completing, composure, patience,* and *compassion.* Trust what the little voice inside is saying.

What you put out attracts the same qualities in those you are dealing with.

(For a self help tool, to be at your peak in every meeting, refer to *Quick Guide II - How to Spot, Mimic and Become a Top Salesperson.*

When you are mindful and apply the four principles listed you are in *the flow* - you are operating at your full intellectual and emotional best (given who you are and the experience you have). To get in *the flow* you have to feel challenged mentally, emotionally or physically.

Take care not to avoid challenges when the avoidance is borne of fear.

Be mindful that, if you feel unchallenged, unstretched, unemotional (as opposed to passionate or composed) you can fall into the 'pit of complacence'. If you don't feel a challenge, create one for yourself.

(**Research Finding:** When top performers are given a target they give themselves at least one 'stretch target', if not more. In doing so, they create the context to place themselves in *the flow*.)

When you are in *the flow*, you will sense when the time is right.

————

Case Study, About Timing:

I was once responsible for closing a one-million-plus pound consulting deal with a new client. We'd given all the information they required to make a decision. They gave us timescales that we would, by contract, need to adhere to. Their decision day had come and gone and no reply was forthcoming.

My company was in a quandary. The resources required to deliver the contract had been lined up but there were calls coming in for their services from elsewhere in the organisation. The time had come where something needed to be done.

I booked a meeting, one Friday afternoon, with the customer's executive sponsor who was responsible for the timely implementation of the project and had authority to sign the contract. After some preliminary chat, I deliberately asked the sponsor if there was any information that I hadn't given him so that he could make a decision.

He said, "No, everything is complete".

I reminded him of the timescales and the significant amount of resources we had lined up. I then asked him if he would sign the contract because if the time slipped any further I might not be able to guarantee that the resources (he'd vetted personally) would be available. (*"High quality consultants are always in demand"*) The sponsor's face turned red.

I was tempted to alleviate his fears but the little voice inside me said, "Shut-up, wait!"

The client stared at his desk. A few seconds later he put the fingers of both hands to his forehead to support his head as he leaned forward on his desktop and stared at its surface. More seconds passed. The sponsor arose, eyes bulging and walked to the window. (He and his company had never signed such a large order for consulting services before). He grabbed a few cross-members of the Venetian blinds at the window and yanked them down so that he could stare through the gap created, into the distance. What seemed an eternity but in reality several seconds passed.

Face aflame, he turned and looked at me straight in the eyes.

After another two seconds, he spoke (at last!), "If this doesn't work, I'll (expletive) kill you, Paul!"

I stared back. It took two seconds for me to compose my reply, "The resources are in place to ensure this project will succeed. Our people together with yours have the know-how to make it succeed."

The client signed the contract.

Later, after the 'thank you' and reassurances, to lighten the moment, I quipped, "And if this project doesn't work, you'll have to join the queue!"

"The Master Mind" and Harmony or Resonance

Every relationship (or group for that matter) has its own spirit. In his book, *The Law of Success,* Napoleon Hill refers to this spirit as *The Master Mind.* Druids refer to it as *Group Spirit.* It is the guiding force in a relationship that manifests for each party the situations, people and events to complete their respective and so unified *journeys to success.*

Napoleon Hill emphasises the importance of *harmony* between two people to invoke the power of *The Master Mind.*

Harmony or Resonance (adapted from my book, *Learn to Love and Be Loved in Return*):

What makes your relationship unique, i.e. impossible (or at least difficult) for others to copy? Answer: the nature and process by which you:

- Tune in to one another.
- Inquire of, advocate and listen to one another.
- Communicate with one voice.

Develop an acute awareness of the meanings and implications of the emotional conflict that you and your business partner have to undergo to achieve the (unified) purpose of the relationship. (Emotional conflict exists because if it were purely a logical or philosophical journey then many people would succeed in business through a purely intellectual process. I know of no-one so blessed.) Be patient.

- Recognise that internal conflict will exist for one or both of you.
- Conflict might arise between you both.
- Overall, recognise purpose (or the *journey*) is not *completed* until both partners achieve it.
- Be prepared, to put aside (relatively petty) self interest for the sake of the *greater good*.
- Complete the journey harmoniously (i.e. free of the consequences of anger, hurt, shame and fear).
- Learn and rise above what holds either of you back, in your respective psyches, together. The resonance between you is what makes your relationship unique.

The intention to create a booklet that can be read within one hour doesn't permit me to go through all of the material I use to help clients 'tune into' others. However, I will give an example to illustrate the importance and effect of how harmony stirs *The Master Mind* into action.

———

Case Study, Resonance: Tuning Into How Another Person Wants to Hear What You Have to Say.

It was early afternoon. I was coaching the European Sales Manager for advanced technologies, for a 'top-five' global IT firm. He was self-profiling his thinking preferences and allocating them to left/right and upper/lower brain working. When one of his direct reports presented to him he liked them to use colour. He preferred diagrams. He liked to think 'big picture'. He had little interest in minutiae or studying spread sheets. He determined that he had a preference for upper/right brain work, i.e. an entrepreneurial spirit that thrives on risk.

He had his half year review the next day with the European GM at the company headquarters. We set about profiling his GM and got a different perspective to his own. As soon as we completed his GM's profile, my client asked if he could terminate the session and then dashed off. He said that something urgent had come up and he would call me in a couple of days.

Two days later he called as promised. *"Paul, I'm sorry for leaving the session half way through but that profiling tool was one of the most valuable techniques you've shown me. You know I had a meeting with the GM whom we determined preferred upper left brain working (i.e. achievement oriented). Well I had thirteen slides of diagrams in glorious colour to show him and needed to change them.*

I went straight home and cut the number of slides down to four: all lists and all in simple black and white.

1. *Annual target and the distribution basis by which I set out to achieve the number.*
2. *Year to date performance and lessons learned.*
3. *Year-end outlook and the logic behind the projected shortfall against target if nothing is done.*
4. *Two options*
   a) *What is needed to make up the shortfall to meet the year-end target.*
   b) *What is needed to overachieve the target.*

I had an hour allocated. I was in and out in thirty minutes. At the end of the session I was asked to join the GM for lunch.

There he told me, 'That was the best presentation I've had this year. I've a job for you. Would you be interested?'"

My client not only got the result he wanted, he got an instant leg up the ladder of his career.

Mindfulness: To Unravel the Mystique and Play the Business Game

The next bit took me a wee while to figure out. It's subtle. You may want to read it a few times because I didn't get it first, second or even the third time around. I hope I can give it justice.

In the context of this book, let's say you define *success* as having a long term sales/client relationship with someone. (*Success* can be any outcome you want in life by the way, e.g. the relationship with your boss, a big house, a job, health, a sales victory, anything.) Alongside *success*, in the future, sits *not-success* (I am deliberately avoiding the *f-word*).

If you're looking to win a sales campaign, you may lose. The closer you get to the decision, the closer you get to *success* and *not-success*. Herein lies *the mindful mystique* to the *journey to success*.

Mindfulness Approach

If you are mindful of, moment by moment, and apply the principles in the preceding sections...

- Demonstrate *faith-in self, passion, curiosity to learn, composure, patience,* and *compassion.*
- Avoid both panicking and reacting out of anger, shame, hurt, and fear - instead, under-react.
- Create harmony and resonance to nurture *The Master Mind.*

- Complete incompletions (when the future presents them to you and in the past you may have reacted negatively) to time.

Then, with these intentions, actions and qualities...

The Mystique

You will induce everything that's incomplete in your approach to your business relationship. This is the future's gift to the present moment. You are given the opportunity to rise above anger, shame, hurt, and fear (borne of the past tense).

When you complete anything in your business approach that is incomplete, it travels into the past and need never return. If you react negatively, i.e. it remains incomplete, it travels into the past before returning to the future - so that you attract the same source of anger, shame, hurt, and fear once again.

The goals of nurturing healthy business relationships may be financial success and kudos but these things are not the purpose.

The real purpose of any relationship, business or otherwise, is the development of self (consciousness) to be the very best at what you do.

When you achieve the above, the goals and purpose become one. You cannot fail because there is no one better and you have no fear of not-success - because...

The Mystique
Genuinely having no fear tells you that not-success no longer exists.

There's a corollary to this. To release your fear you need to approach not-success. Which is why I encourage you to...

Include not-success as well as success in what you want.

Get it?

When You Achieve Business Success but Not Its Purpose

Case Study, Fear in Business (extract from *Defrag your Soul*)

I coached a UK General Manager of a global software firm. He'd been in his post for just over a year. He was very experienced and excellent at corporate account, business-to-business, selling. In the current economic climate he felt exhausted. He told how he spent the vast majority of his time chasing 'big-ticket sales contracts' personally. He feared that if he didn't make his company's sales targets then he would be fired. So he took it upon himself to engage personally in selling the really big deals, whilst his salespeople stood and watched from the side.

He didn't allow himself time to focus on strategic changes he wanted to make, so that the company would become more competitive in the long term. Come the end of his first year in post, the UK company made its sales target. But, the General Manager felt unfulfilled. He was using "less than 5% of my creative skills". He felt he had no option but to get up and do it again. He feared if he left the selling to others, they wouldn't do the job properly. He feared to let go. So the coaching we went through focused on releasing his fears.

_____ End of Case Study

Actions borne of fear, even when hugely successful, do not release that fear. They simply keep that fear in abeyance. Your journey remains incomplete.

Let's get back to the business relationship you want. If you apply and only apply *faith-in self, passion, curiosity to learn, composure, patience, compassion,* and *completeness* to your quest then you are on the right track to *success*. What do I mean by *completeness*?

Completeness means acknowledgement of any anger, hurt, shame, and fear that the image of *not-success* presents you. If you attempt to avoid *not-success* through thoughts, deeds and words borne of anger, hurt, shame, or fear, you are denying yourself the opportunity to release these negative emotions; they control you. But they are not the 'real you', they are a shadow that hides the 'real you' from you - and those you come into contact with.

Nor does it serve your *purpose* to deny these negative feelings. For you cannot release what you do not acknowledge to possess.

Instead, your purpose is served initially by allowing these negative emotions to be. Allow yourself to be okay with them so that you can deal with them (e.g. dealing with sales objections). I know from personal experience that when I have been seriously upset, this has been a very difficult if not an impossible task right there, then, in the moment. It's taken me a lot of practice to 'stay cool' during times when I feel extremely hurt or fearful. I'm better at it these days, not perfect. Here's what I do to stay cool (when I remember to!)...

(**When you have an upset...**) In practical terms if you feel anger, hurt, shame, or fear welling up within you...

1. Close your eyes and take two or three deep breaths.
2. Place the negative emotions in an imaginary bubble in front you.
3. Breathe light into the bubble through your *Third Eye* or *Brow Centre*, just above and between your eyebrows until some level of composure returns to you.

Composure is (also) the ability to neither feed nor fight the most negative of emotions: anger, hurt, shame, and fear when under duress.

The more you practise, the stronger your imagination, the quicker the time to releasing the negative emotion.

That upon which light shines becomes that light
St Paul

Recite an affirmation to help you avoid feeding or fighting the negative emotion. For example, I recite the phrase...

"I create passion and composure - and include every outcome (i.e. success and not-success)."

... as I shine light into my imaginary bubble of fear.

Towards A Better Business World

When you strive to be a top performer the way top performers do, i.e. through *mindfulness*, you create better business relationships. Supreme business success is forged from supreme business relationships. Top performers forge their relationships through truth, the quest for 'personal *completeness*'.

Imagine the whole world of business practising the release of anger, hurt, shame, and fear. Every relationship between two or more people (organisations or nations) would serve a purpose where no one could fail; a utopia where every unanswered question not only has, but becomes, a purpose.

You have the power to create your part in such a business world.

Without anger, hurt, shame, and fear, that which remains is the highest vibration a human can aspire to, joy and fulfilment.

The goal of business is to make money and its purpose is to make life joyful and fulfilling.

That's the game, the *Business Game* which is integral to the *Game of Life*.

(End of main body of article)

Thank you...

...For purchasing this booklet. If you'd like further information about the variety of services I engage in, please visit these websites...

http://paulcburr.com/ ~ extensive and ethereal blog-site that combines business with ancient wisdom

http://www.facebook.com/PaulCBurr ~ over 15,000 followers

http://twitter.com/paulburr

www.cotoco.com ~ for brilliant 'wisdom- transfer' solutions; to pass on what the top performers in your organisation do differently from the moderate performers. Please mention this book should you contact *Cotoco*.

Or mailto: doctapaul@paulcburr.com

About me, Paul C Burr

I equip executives, sales people and personal clients to raise their 'game' by 30%+ in a matter of weeks, sometimes days.

Business Client: *"I have worked with Paul periodically over the past 8 years to gain solutions to a number of people issues / opportunities. If you are looking for a Personal Coach to make a High Performer / High Performing Team even better (particularly a senior player) – I would not hesitate to recommend him."* - Sandra Ventre, Management Development Director, Reckitt Benckiser (now with Qantas)

Private Client: *"You have been so instrumental in the positive changes in my life, I set quite a few goals, and one by one my goals are being achieved, thanks to you, showing me how."* - Debbie (via Skype) Cape Town, South Africa.

Partial Client List: Accenture, Avery Dennison, Bevan Ashford, Bombardier, BP Marine, Cambridge Technology Partners, Castrol, Charles Burton (European Amateur Natural Bodybuilding Champion), Cisco, Cotoco, CSC, Dept of Trade & Industry (private client), Dixons Group, DTZ, Erevena, Grace Construction, IBM, Newcastle City Council, Northumbria University, Prudential, Reckitt Benckiser, SHL, Staffware (now part of Tibco), United Biscuits, Xerox, Youthforce

The Skills and Passions in Me

Life doesn't get better by chance; it gets better by change.

And change is a journey that's two parts emotional to one part intellectual.

Most of us don't achieve what we set out to achieve at the first attempt. If the outcomes you sought were down to a purely intellectual exercise then you would have achieved them already - would you not? Whether you're a top or moderate performer (or underperforming right now) - every change you make in life is a journey, two parts emotional to one part intellectual. We are twice as likely to hold ourselves back because of self-imposed limiting beliefs we hold about ourselves, our organisation or customers, as opposed to intellectual problems. Put simply, I equip people to tackle challenging emotional journeys; to go beyond the limits to success they impose on themselves and others.

Corporate clients use me as a 'business coach', personal clients probably see me as more of an 'energy healer'. In both cases I help clients to cultivate and apply their innate willpower, imagination, courage and creativity to achieve the business and personal outcomes they seek.

I have over thirty-five years of B2B corporate sales and management experience, sixteen years of which overlap with my business and personal coaching work. I have a PhD in Statistics and a First Class Honours Degree in Mathematics. I'm qualified as a Master Practitioner in NLP, this/past life regression and hypnotherapy.

I give talks (and appear on talk shows) on selling, executive coaching, Neuro-Linguistic Programming (NLP), ancient wisdom, football and more ethereal subjects – sometimes to the same audience!

I write books, blogs and am now partway through a series of business articles based upon my own original research, experience and observations in corporate and small/medium sized businesses.

I study and practice ancient wisdom, astrology, casting runes, dowsing, the I Ching and the Tarot.

I love listening to music – rock, jazz, country... you name it. I sing a bit too.

I'm a passionate football fan of Newcastle United Football Club, in "Geordieland", in The North-East of England.

My Promise:

The material I use is powerful, very powerful. I know of nothing quicker or more effective. It's non-mainstream - which means you get non-mainstream results.

The Author in Me...

Quick Guides to Business, Volumes I - VII

Quick Guide: How Top Salespeople Sell (for new or seasoned sales professionals, managers and CEOs) Number 1 in a series of articles by Paul C Burr PhD	Quick Guide II: How to Spot, Mimic and Become a Top Salesperson (for new or seasoned sales professionals, managers and CEOs) Number 2 in a series of articles by Paul C Burr PhD	Quick Guide III: How to Bridge the Pillars of Successful Business Relationships (for CEOs, salespeople and everyone in between) Number 3 in a series of articles by Paul C Burr PhD
Quick Guide IV: A Scorecard that Accounts for Mindfulness in Business (A simple product and process for CEOs, programme managers and anyone wishing to visualise and measure personal, team or corporate success.) Number 4 in a series of articles by Paul C Burr PhD	Quick Guide V: How to Apply Mindfulness to Business Relationships Number 5 in a series of articles by Paul C Burr PhD	Quick Guide VI: How to Sell Coaching Number 6 in a series of articles by Paul C Burr PhD
Quick Guide VII: A Top-notch, Sales-Relationships, Account Management Template Number 7 in a series of articles by **Paul C Burr PhD**		

"...a really impressive series"

Professor John Ditch

Quick Guide – How Top Salespeople Sell

"...a must read for both novice salespeople and the experienced...." - Author, Chiahou Zhang

"I loved it... it was great. I've encouraged many of my directors to buy a copy as it's very pertinent to my company" - paraphrased from a top performing B2B salesperson for a global IT Services organisation

"I work for a large American IT company, and can say this is a hugely powerful book to articulate what is required to get to Board level. To really understand what the CEO and C level executive summarise as valuable and impactful, and in a condensed easy-to-digest format, is phenomenal. I find Paul C Burr's style of writing easier to digest and apply in any sales situation; it crystallises where the true business value add is delivered and how you really have strategic partnerships. I have just got number 2 book and look forward to reading this with excitement - which is saying something as my concentration span can be limited. Thank you." - Amy Lambkin, 5-stars, book review

Quick Guide II - How to Spot, Mimic and Become a Top Salesperson

Learn to Love and Be Loved in Return

"Uplifting: this is one of those books that arrives in your life at just the right time, when you need it most. The author is able to convey a very deep and meaningful message in an easy to read and understand format with a step by step guide on how to achieve this. The best type of love is unconditional and what better place to start than with yourself." - Rhedd, 5-stars, book review

2012: a twist in the tail, a novel with spiritual insights

"This is a compelling story for our troubled times. Paul C Burr writes with passion and compassion about moral uncertainties and the quest for salvation and spiritual fulfilment. Go with the flow, trust your inner-self and enjoy this humane and optimistic tale." - Professor John Ditch, York, UK.

"This is a gripping read - beautiful, insightful and very enjoyable. I found phrases and thoughts staying with me, and becoming part of my understanding of the world." - Caroline Eveleigh, *Getting to Excellent*

Defrag your Soul

"You should be proud of DYS Paul. I think it is amazing and I'm still thinking hard about what you've written." - Amanda Giles, Author

"DYS whispered to me, 'take heart, be aware, let your journey this far nourish your inner self to be at peace, to love and to shine as your journey continues'." - Penelope Walsh, Book Review

The Mystique to the Game of Life (and Unrequited Love)

The Mystique to the Game of Life (and Unrequited Love)

Mindfulness Exercises in Relationships Series, No 1

Paul C Burr PhD

"Revelatory - the Mystique to the Game of Life drew me in. I wanted to carry on reading as much as I wanted to stop and do the exercises! It struck a number of chords with me, and just through reading the book I became aware of some very important

things - habits, conditioning, behaviours - that I needed to address to make my life and my relationships happier and healthier. The author has a way of writing that reaches deep down into your heart; it gets you in that feeling place. His writing is more than words on a page. It's more a guide that leads us to recognise, deal with and move on from whatever may be holding us back." - Amazon 5 star review

For The Love of Lilith & How to Put Love into Practice: (and Non-attach Yourself To It)

"For the Love of Lilith is a powerful tool to enhance the awareness, appreciation and enjoyment of living and loving in harmony. It is a book that can be used to strengthen and reinforce areas of my life and make sense of the non-sense that can accompany me in matters of the heart." - Amazon 5 star review

...Has the deep understanding of the shadow side of the female, knowing of the fear, shame, anger and sadness of being abandoned and how to turn these feelings into light and love.

If you like this one you will love "Defrag your Soul" as well. - Amazon 5 star review

How to Be a Friend of the Devil Within